CW00386529

TAJ
MAHAL

© Crest Publishing House
First published 2000

Published by Crest Publishing House
G2, 16 Ansari Road, Darya Ganj,
New Delhi 110002
Ph: (011) 3252366, 3264748 Fax: (011) 3278469
E-mail: sethidel@ndf.vsnl.net.in

Introduction: Anees Jung
Edited by: Kishore Singh
Photographs: Gopi Gajwani
Text: © Himalayan Books
Photographs: ©Gopi Gajwani
Designed by: Yogesh Gajwani and Suraksha Gajwani

ISBN 81-242-0185-4

Mumtaz Mahal

Shah Jahan

For many, India is the Taj Mahal. With it is associated the story of a love between a man and a woman, in this case a king and his queen. 'It is too pure, too holy to be the work of human hands,' said one medieval writer. 'Angels must have brought it from heaven and a glass case should be thrown over it to preserve it from every breath of air.' Through the centuries the Taj has been the most exquisite specimen of human architecture and the most gorgeous romance of wedded love.

Each time I have seen and sensed the Taj I have wondered about Shah Jahan, the man who made it possible. He was an emperor and a powerful one, who had the time and inclination to also be a man. He was married to Mumtaz-uz-Zamani, who received from him the title of Mumtaz Mahal, at the age of 20. She bore him 14 children, and died giving birth to the last, a daughter. At the time of her death, there were no more than 20 white hairs in the king's beard, it is said. In three days, his head turned white. He went into mourning for two years — wore white, gave up his jewels, used no perfumes, heard no music. In 18 years, at the cost of three million sterling, he built her a mausoleum, calling it the Taj Mahal.

Shah Jahan was fifth in line of the Mughals who first arrived in India with Babar. Babar not only conquered Hindustan but stayed on to make it his home. He settled in Agra, on the banks of the Jamuna, creating for himself a garden that he called Gul Afshan (gold scattering), known today as Ram Bagh. The most creative period in Mughal history were the years between 1526 and 1657 that spanned the period of the first five emperors: Babar, Humayun, Akbar, Jehangir and Shah Jahan. What Babar began was strengthened by his grandson Akbar, and embellished to a new zenith by Akbar's grandson Shah Jahan. Father Monserrate, a Jesuit priest who saw Agra in 1580, noted that 'the city was famous for its mild climate, its fertile soil, its great river, its beautiful gardens; its fame spread to the end of the earth'. The city, as he described it, was four miles long and two miles broad. Despite the heat and the hot desiccating winds, there were fruits and flowers and gardens. 'The city of Agra is surrounded by gardens,' wrote Niccolao Manucci, a Venetian who served as a gunner in the Mughal army. 'The fortress is placed on the bank of the river, with a ditch that can be filled with water from the river. On both sides, the fortress is adorned with beautiful palaces for the blood-royal and the grandees.'

What was Agra like before the first Mughal made it his home? Less than 500 years ago it was a massive mound of earth rising above the banks of the river Jamuna. Historians tell a story, rooted perhaps in legend, that it was first discovered in its Muslim incarnation by the Pathan king, Sikander Lodi. The Sultan is said to have sent a party of officials to explore the banks of the river, and recommend a site suitable for the building of a new city. The officials left Delhi in boats, proceeded along the banks and discovered the site where the city now stands. The king is said to have arrived himself to inspect the site. When he observed two eminent mounds on the banks he asked the *nayak* of the royal barge which of the two would be suitable. The *nayak* replied "That which is *age-rah*," meaning that which is in advance on the way. "Then let the name of the town be Age-rah," said the king. Agra became the seat of his government and grew in importance, becoming a grand resort of learned men from Persia, Arabia and Bokhara.

Legends take us back deeper into antiquity. In the sacred region of Jamuna, Vyasa is said to have been born. He was the arranger of the Vedas and was the author of the epic Mahabharata. The Hindu origins of Agra are traced to the very root of its name *agu*, which in Sanskrit means prior or first. Here, it is said, was the first of the many groves where the God-king Krishna played and lived. Around Agra still flourish the towns associated with the Krishna legend — Mathura and Vrindaban, Gokul, Goverdhan and

Nandgaon. Linked to Agra by the sacred river, these ancient towns form the region known as Brajbhoomi.

What is Agra today? It is neither the city which the Mughals had turned into a grand garden resort, nor is it that ancient place with a fort which Raja Kans, the ruler of Mathura, is believed to have chosen to confine those who incurred his wrath, and which in course of time turned into the famous state prison. Today, it is hardly more than a sprawling tinsel town that had once been beautifully assembled around the domes and minarets of the Mughals. Besides the river Jamuna that flows discreetly at the edges of its burgeoning landscapes, there is little that is mystical about the city as one begins to discover it. What remains of its grandeur is 'protected'. Government departments are the custodians of its tombs and mosques, its palaces, pavilions and forts. Strong and solid, they silently testify to the gallantry of life that they once contained.

Few memorials of Babar's short and brilliant reign survive in Agra today, except the historic road, the Ram Bagh which he created, and Zuhara Bagh that carries vestiges of a garden house that is said to have belonged to his daughter. Across from the Taj Mahal are traces of the foundations of a city he had begun to build. Disenchanted by the desolation of the country, Babar had noted in his memoirs: 'One of the chief defects of Hindustan is the want of artificial water courses. I had intended, wherever I may fix my residence, to construct water wheels to produce an artificial stream and to lay out an elegant and regularly planned pleasure ground. Shortly after coming to Agra I passed the Jamuna with this object in view, and examined the country to pitch upon a fit spot for a garden. The whole was so ugly and detestable that I repassed the river quite repulsed and disgusted. In consequence of the want of beauty and the disagreeable aspect of the country, I gave up my intention of making a *char bagh* (garden house); but as no better situation presented itself near Agra I was finally compelled to make the best of this same spot... In every corner I planted suitable gardens, in every garden I sowed roses and narcissus regularly and in beds corresponding to each other. We were annoyed by three things in Hindustan, one was its heat, another the strong winds and the third its dust. Baths were the means of removing all three inconveniences."

The 20-year-old Humayun who succeeded Babur left no memorials in Agra. A handsome mosque which he had begun to construct immediately after succession stands desolate in a nearby village called Kachpura. Few of the denizens know its history. It is a sacred place they say. Incense is lit in its dark enclosure every Thursday. Humayun did not complete the mosque nor pray in it.

The gardens the Mughal kings planned on earth were only a preparation for the ultimate *bahisht* in heaven. Each garden I visit in Agra is a reminder of that ideal — whether it is the tomb of Akbar in Sikandra, the resplendent Itmad-ul-Daula, or the Taj Mahal. Over the simple grave where

Akbar lies buried rises the grand mausoleum in raging pink sandstone. In the simplicity and silence of the chamber lie the mortal remains of a great emperor. Over the simple stone grave the red colour of sandstone structures is broken by the white marble of the delicate minarets and the glazed blue shimmer of the designs. Open to the sky, in the centre of the marble enclosure of the highest storey, is the second tombstone, exactly in the same position as the one in the lowest terrace which represents the actual tomb. The centre of white marble is carved in an arabesque of leaves and blossoms. Inscribed on either side of the tombstone are the 99 attributes of God.

According to some historians, the head of Akbar's grave, unlike that of other tombs, is not turned towards Mecca but towards the rising sun. It is said that Akbar worshipped the sun four times a day as the greatest light. He adapted costumes of seven different colours which he wore on the seven days of the week according to the seven colours of the seven planets. And he allowed himself to be worshipped as a deity. When he appeared each morning at the window of his palace, multitudes prostrated before him in a *sijda*, an act which he banished, substituting in its place *zamin bosi* or kissing the ground. Women brought their sick children to receive his benediction and on recovery offered him gifts. They brought cups of water. He exposed it to the sun, breathed into it and gave it back to be sipped. He abstained, like the Hindus, from beef; even gave up garlic, onions and the wearing of a beard in the Muslim fashion. The reading and learning of Arabic by the common people that caused mischief mongering, was discouraged. Instead, the study of philosophy, astronomy, medicine, mathematics, history and poetry was encouraged. A Jesuit priest who visited Akbar's court reports: 'The emperor can neither read nor write but is extremely eager after knowledge and always has learned men about him whom he invites to discuss or to narrate to him.' He was gifted with a marvellous memory and judgement, was witty and full of humour.

Jehangir was born after Akbar's visit to the village of Sikri to meet the great Sufi saint Salim Chisti, who advised him to make Sikri his home. 'My father,' writes Jehangir, 'regarding Sikri, my birthplace, as fortunate to himself, made it his capital, and in the course of 14 or 15 years, the hills and deserts which abounded in beast of prey, became converted into a city comprising numerous gardens, elegant edifices and pavilions. After the conquest of Gujarat, the village was named Fatehpur (the town of victory).' The glory of this new capital was short-lived. After holding court here for 17 years, Akbar returned to Agra. Some say that it was shortage of water; others feel that the saint was being disturbed by the bustle of the new city and felt that either he or Akbar must go. 'Then, let it be your servant,' said the emperor. Deserted for a few hundred years now, the city stands yearning for people.

Besides Fatehpur Sikri, Akbar built the modern city of

Agra across from the site where his grandfather, Babar, built his garden. The city was then named after him, Akbarabad. In his autobiography, Jehangir gives an account of the old Agra and the foundations of the new city laid by Akbar. 'Agra is one of the most ancient and populous cities of Hindustan. It had an old fort on the bank of the Jamuna but my father, before my birth, built on its site a fort of red sandstone, so magnificent that men who have travelled through the world maintain that they have seen the like of it nowhere.' One enters the fort through the Delhi Gate, then the elephant gate, flanked by two stone elephants, and then the Naubat Khana where the royal drums were played to announce the emperor's arrival or departure. From the gate one gets a good view of the fort and beyond the walls, across the Jamuna, the fine vision of the Taj and, on the left, the tomb of Itmad-ul-Daula. Within the fort are the palaces of Shah Jehan and Jehangir, the Samman Burj of Nur Jehan and the Khas Mahal and Anguri Bagh of the ladies. The most exquisite, perhaps, is the Moti Masjid, appropriately called the Pearl Mosque, with its fine arcades. Through the Mina Bazaar of the old marketplace, the gateway opens into the wide courtyard of Diwan-i-Am, where the emperor daily gave audience, met ambassadors and administered justice.

On the terrace in front of Diwan-i-Khas, the private hall, is the throne of black marble where Jehangir is said to have watched elephant fights and river sports. Conspicuous are the baths or the *hamams* which the Mughals constructed, where water was brought up from the well, 70 feet below. The Jehangiri Mahal was planned by Akbar in a style that evolved with Fatehpur before the new element came in the Mughal architecture of Itmad-ul-Daula. Both these styles exist side by side at the Agra Fort.

In 1608, Captain Hawkins waited on Jehangir with a letter from James the First of England. Europeans had free access to his palace. The emperor drank with them all night, even in the month of Ramadan; so different from his father who spent long hours learning from scholars and philosophers. Hawkins describes a day in the life of Jehangir: 'In the morning, at daybreak, the emperor turned his face towards Mecca and chanted different names of God on a string of pearls. He then appeared at the *jharokha* (window) to receive the salutations of the multitudes. This time, he went to sleep for two hours more and then took his meals with the ladies of the seraglio. At noon he showed himself at the balcony and sat there until three o'clock to witness pastimes by men and beast. In the evening, the emperor was in the *ghusl khana* or private room where ministers and amirs waited on His Majesty and business of the state was transacted. A rope with ringing bells was fastened to a pillar in the king's chamber. Any poor man who demanded justice pulled it, hearing which the king called him and gave him justice.'

Hawkins drank with Jehangir in the *ghusl khana*. Sir Thomas Roe brought presents to Jehangir from the King of England, which included an English coach. Jehangir gave it to his favourite wife, Nur Mahal. She exercised a great influence on him. Money was coined in her name. The part of the palace where she lived still stands in the Agra Fort, known as Samman Burj or Jasmine Bower. It bears the fine designs which she personally sketched and supervised. She is said to have set new trends in fashion and jewellery in the harem. In the tomb of Itmad-ul-Daula that she built for her father, there is a design of a flower vase in which is painted her image, while on a goblet of wine is painted the portrait of her husband.

It was Shah Jahan, the son of Jehangir, who gave to Agra the Taj Mahal which was to become synonymous not only with one city and one age but with a world of all times. A king's monument of grief was turned into a wonder of the world.

In keeping with the Tartar, and later the Mughal tradition, before the tomb came the garden. Its flowers and fruits were the emblems of life; the solemn cypress trees symbolised death and eternity. The planning of the Taj took several years. From drawings of the most celebrated buildings, a design given by Ustad Tsa (a Byzantine Turk or a native of Shiraz) was accepted. Master builders came from all parts of the world; chief masons from Baghdad and Delhi, dome builders from Turkey, mosaic workers from Kanouj and calligraphers from Shiraz. From Jaipur came the marble, from Fatehpur Sikri the red sandstone, from Punjab jasper, from Tibet turquoise, from China jade and crystal, from Arabia coral, and from Persia onyx and amethyst. Twenty thousand men were employed in the construction, and it took 18 years to create the wonder.

Shah Jahan died gazing at his monument to love from a chamber in Agra Fort. With his death the court lost its splendour and Agra slowly slipped into obscurity. Its role in history diminished in the reign of his son Aurangzeb, who was busy with his exploits in the Deccan. In 1739,

Nadir Shah of Persia sacked Delhi and later Agra, taking away with him the Peacock Throne of Shah Jahan. In 1764, the Jats of Bharatpur captured Agra, looted the Taj and the palaces of the Fort. In 1803, Agra was taken by the British.

Agra bustles today like any other burgeoning town in India. Here and there one senses a powerful tug of organic continuity with a past that was bold and vibrant. I felt it at the tomb of Akbar, watching a man and a woman praying to a dead king; I sensed it in the serenity of the Kailash Temple on the banks of a sacred river; I encountered it in the dedicated fact of the *qadim* at the Taj and in the vigour of an artisan's hands who sat below the monument carving the white marble with a black stone leaf; I was swept away by the warmth of a marriage procession in the old Kinari Bazaar which I was invited to join as a stranger. I exulted in it spaciously, walking through the planned gardens of the dead Mughals in whose plan the end of all life was one — the garden of paradise!

The Taj Mahal, one of the most enduring monuments of the world, was built as a symbol of an emperor's love.

From every angle, the Taj Mahal has a symmetry that is pleasing, a sense of proportion that is manifest in even the detailed inlay on its surface.

Made entirely of marble carried from nearby
Makrana, the tomb is amazingly simple in its details,
though the craftsmanship is exquisite.
Overleaf: Details from the calligraphy.

Preceding pages: Silhouette of the gateway to the Taj.
These pages: Different moods of the Taj Mahal, pearly in
the early dawn, bathed in a rosy glow in the morning,
and shining bright in the noonday sun. Each visit
enhances its mystery, even as it reveals itself further.

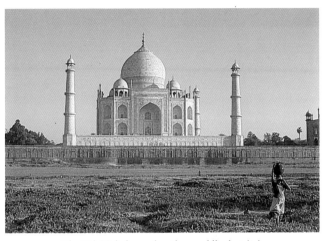

The Taj Mahal may be other-worldly, but it is
rooted in the soil of Agra, a part of the life of the people who
work in the fields that surround it.

*Nothing reflects the magnificence of the Taj Mahal as much as water,
whether in the form of the flowing waters of the river on whose banks it is
built, or in the channels that form a part of its garden complex.*

The architecture of the Taj Mahal may have been supervised by Shah Jahan, but some of the keenest minds and sharpest intellects from around the world participated in its final making.

Preceding pages: A sandstone mosque flanks the Taj to one side. The final resting place of Nur Jahan's father (left), and of Mumtaz Mahal and Shah Jahan with its marble screen that surrounds their graves (top).

*The Taj Mahal can be glimpsed from
Agra Fort; it was probably
from here that its builder had his last
view from his apartment where he was
imprisoned by his son.*

The red sandstone walls of Agra Fort offer a rugged frame for the delicate, almost feminine beauty of the Taj Mahal. It was from here that Shah Jahan supervised the building of this magnificent tomb.

*From these apatments, Mumtaz Mahal must have
gazed across the banks of the Yamuna, little realising that
her tomb would be built on the same spot.*

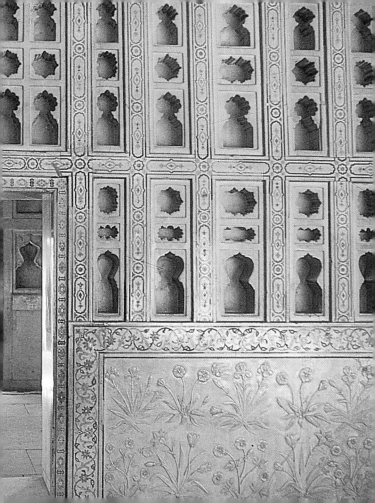

*Preceding pages and these pages: Agra Fort was the centre of
Mughal power for several centuries, and was
added to by all the emperors who built its different parts.*

*The pillars and arches of the audience halls
at Agra Fort are similar to those of Red Fort in Delhi,
and the inlay work shares the same, exquisite details.*

These pages and overleaf: The ramparts of Agra Fort symbolised both pomp and power, the seat for one of the most important empires of the medieval world. The Mughals ruled over Hindustan from here, as well as from their forts in Delhi and Lahore, occupying them according to the strategic requirement of their defence campaigns.

*The Itmad-ud-Daula is an exquisite building,
a tomb designed by Empress Nur Jehan in the memory
of her father, an influential courtier.*

The fine inlay motifs, the small-jewel-box casket shape,
and the play of light and shade at Itmad-ud-Daula
owes its aesthetics to Nur Jehan's design.

*Sikandra is the tomb of Emperor Akbar,
begun by him in his lifetime but
completed by his successor, Emperor
Jehangir, who is also responsible for its
amazing mosaic work.*

If the Taj Mahal took two decades to build, Dayal Bagh, on Agra's outskirts, is a marble wonder that has been under construction for almost a century, and is still far from completion.

The city of Fatehpur Sikri, just beyond Agra, is among the most ambitious building projects undertaken by the Mughals, and one of their most splendid. Akbar's city, however, was abandoned a few years after its occupation.

The sandstone walls and cracked courtyards of Fatehpur Sikri hold on to nostlagic memories of a time when it was the Mughal capital for a brief while.

Preceding pages and these pages: The sculpturing at Fatehpur Sikri uses geometrical and floral motifs to create delicate patterns, though the architecture itself has a rugged robustness.

95

*Fatehpur Sikri was raised as a new city
in thanksgiving to Salim Chishti, a holy man whose tomb
within the complex continues to attract visitors who believe he
still has the power to grant boons.*

The tomb of Salim Chishti is probably the most delicate structure in Fatehpur Sikri, with marble used to create ornate patterns for a saint who otherwise led an extremely austere life.

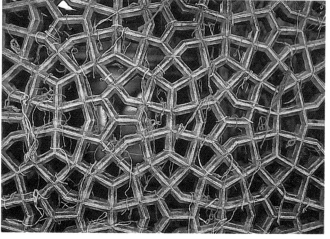

People who come to the tomb of Salim Chishti tie threads to remind him of their desires, and then come to untie them once their wishes have been fulfilled.

The Taj Mahal casts its long shadow not only through history, but over the town of Agra too, its presence unmistakable and omnipresent.

*Built along the banks of the Yamuna,
the Taj Mahal is surrounded by gardens, reminiscent of the tradition
of paradise in Tartar folklore.*

Though the memorial was built by an emperor, the Taj Mahal touches the heart of every person who comes close to it, a reminder that love is immortal and everlasting.

The sun may have set on the Mughal dynasty, but the Taj Mahal still stands as a reminder not only of the empire but also of the emperors who once ruled here — with their minds, and hearts.